My Cat Becomes a Self-Publisher
A Cat's Wisdom to Self-Publishing

Winnie Fontaine, Floofy the Cat

Souls Press Limited

Copyright © 2023 by Souls Press Limited

All rights reserved.

No portion of this book may be reproduced in any form without written permission from the publisher or author, except as permitted by U.S. copyright law.

This publication is designed to provide accurate and authoritative information in regard to the subject matter covered. It is sold with the understanding that neither the author nor the publisher is engaged in rendering legal, investment, accounting or other professional services. While the publisher and author have used their best efforts in preparing this book, they make no representations or warranties with respect to the accuracy or completeness of the contents of this book and specifically disclaim any implied warranties of merchantability or fitness for a particular purpose. No warranty may be created or extended by sales representatives or written sales materials. The advice and strategies contained herein may not be suitable for your situation. You should consult with a professional when appropriate. Neither the publisher nor the author shall be liable for any loss of profit or any other commercial damages, including but not limited to special, incidental, consequential, personal, or other damages.

First edition 2023

ISBN: 978-1-7386088-0-5 (paperback)

ISBN: 978-1-7386088-2-9 (eBook)

Dedication

First and foremost, I want to extend my deepest gratitude and heartfelt thanks to the brilliant self-publishing gurus who have generously shared their wisdom through countless YouTube videos. You are the guiding stars in this magical world of self-publishing.

This book is dedicated not only to the masterminds, but to every self-publisher who is fearlessly shaping history with their words and creativity.

In the days of yore, the mere thought of publishing my own book and sharing it with readers across the globe seemed like a distant dream. Yet here I stand, in awe of the incredible journey.

As an avid fan of Marvel movies, particularly the captivating story of the X-Men, I find myself envisioning a world where I, like Professor X, connect with fellow self-publishing mutants from every corner of the world via this book.

To each and every one of you who has inspired me on this exhilarating expedition, my gratitude knows no bounds.

To all indie writers, publishers, and scribes who breathe life into the written word, you are the true heroes. I hold you in the highest regard, with unwavering respect for your craft. May your path be paved with boundless success.

With utmost sincerity and gratitude,

Winnie Fontaine and Floofy

To all indie writers, publishers, and scribes who breathe life into the written word, you are the true heroes.

Contents

Introduction	1
1. Should I Quit Publishing?	5
A Wake-Up Call from Floofy	
Bonus Page	16
2. Defining Your Unique Proposition	19
An Introduction to Floofy	
Finding Your Unique Proposition	
Embracing the Company of Those You Can Delight	
Sharpening Your Senses	
3. Navigate Your Own Route	35
Finding Your Unique Route	
Embracing Setbacks with a Roaring Cat-titude	
Sustaining the Everlasting Curiosity	
Nurturing Your Cat-Like Resilience	
4. Finding Your Purr-Suit	55
Embracing Patience and Observance	
Retrieving Your Needle in the Haystack	
Cultivating an Invaluable Relationship with Readers	

    Unveiling the Wisdom of Reader Bonding

5. Do It for Yourself and You Mean It   75
    Doing It for Yourself
    Enjoying the Process
    Unleashing Your Unquenchable Hunter Passion
    Building Your Brand

6. Choosing Your Battle   97
    Picking Your Fight
    Recharging and Restoring
    Herding Cats and Dogs

Conclusion   115

About the Author   120

Calling for ARC Readers   122

Bonus Page   123

References   124

Introduction

Once upon a time, there was a tale that went beyond what met the eyes. Friends, I have a story to tell you! It's the wild and wacky journey of how my cat became an indie author, or rather, a co-author (since she's not the greatest at typing). Believe it or not, this is not some silly gimmick. Floofy, my four-year-old tortoiseshell wonder, is an actual, bona fide contributor to this book.

Now, let me introduce myself. I'm Winnie, the fortunate human who stumbled upon Floofy's feline brilliance. It all began in 2019 when I decided to embark on a life-altering visit to the SPCA. Picture a room filled with adorable kittens, each posing like debutantes at a college ball, longing for the perfect invitation. But guess what? Floofy didn't play by the rules.

While the others were busy showcasing their picture-perfect poses, our little rebel, with a bound of pure determination, sprang onto the fence of her cage, extending her tiny paw outside the cage as if to say, "Hey, you! Yeah, you! Choose me, human!" How could I resist such a spunky and unconventional kitty? Okay, maybe tortoiseshells aren't everyone's cup of tea, but trust me, once you lay eyes on their funky patterns and unique personalities, you'll be smitten. I mean, when Floofy curls up for a nap, it's like a riddle: Where's her head? Where's her tail? There's some debate going on about Floofy's fur color classification. Is she a calico? Is she a tortie? I scoured the internet and still couldn't come to a conclusion. But let me tell you, those who have had the pleasure of knowing Floofy can all agree on one thing: she's got a tortitude that could rival even the sassiest of cats!

But enough about the fluff! Let's get down to the key part. Floofy is ready to join me in the world of writing, one paw at a time. This book isn't your typical fiction story, mind you. No, no. It's a blend of humor, life wisdom, and all the quirky challenges of self-publishing. Think of it as a philosophical and mental adventure wrapped in a thin blanket of humorous.

So join us, my friend, as Floofy and I take you on a whimsical ride through the ups and downs of a cat's philosopher dreams and a human's quest for wisdom in self-publishing. Get ready to chuckle, ponder, and maybe even find a nugget of wisdom hidden behind those whiskers.

MY CAT BECOMES A SELF-PUBLISHER

Chapter 1
Should I Quit Publishing?

"I quit when opportunities dwindle, or exhaustion dims my feline fire. But fear not, for I'll recharge and pounce again tomorrow!"

Floofy, The Philosopher Cat

A Wake-Up Call from Floofy

Like many self-publishers, my journey started after encountering a super inspiring YouTube video that revealed to me a lot of upsides of self-publishing, including consistent flows of passive income, geographical flexibility, unrestricted retirement age, autonomous working hours, and many more. Sounds familiar?

Then I searched for more YouTube videos, watching many more successful self-publishers share their success stories. There are young mothers, a self-made millionaire in his twenties, a girl who looks like a teenager, or at most in her early twenties, who made multiple five-figures with just one lined journal, and many more who have quit their full-time jobs after generating enough regular income through Amazon KDP. Then I told myself, if they can, I can do that too.

Then now you probably know what happened afterward. I enrolled in a course that I found to be highly relevant and valuable. I equipped myself with crucial knowledge and invaluable advice. I subscribed myself to all necessary tools and services, including a couple of keyword research tools, an auto-email responder, a grammar checker, a plagiarism checker, an A.I. detector, and you name the rest. I also registered an LLC, a matching domain, and a Virtual Mailbox.

MY CAT BECOMES A SELF-PUBLISHER

Self-publishing has its share of challenges, so prepare yourself. I won't waste your time by stating the obvious; we're all aware of how difficult this work is. Whether you are writing the book yourself or hiring ghostwriters, there are still many challenges to overcome, such as maintaining effective communication with freelancers, proofreading, editing, formatting, and choosing the appropriate book cover designs. These, however, are the easy parts! Cue the laughter music, please!

Let's move on to the meat of self-publishing: promotion, gathering book reviews, building a mailing list, etc. It's like diving head-first into a sea of hungry piranhas. Fun, right? Well, not exactly. After months of burning the midnight oil, pouring my heart, soul, and every penny I could find into my books, I reached a tipping point. You know that magical moment where you contemplate quitting and running off to join a circus!

Why, you asked? Okay, let's do some quick math. I've put in a lot of money and sweat and tears, like a person training for a marathon. But then the truth hits me like a plot twist: I haven't even made enough to buy a pair of cool socks. Seriously, besides book production, I spent a small fortune on Amazon ads, and what's the grand payoff after six months? A meager trickle of income that barely covers a fancy meal at the local taco truck.

Oh, but wait, it gets better. Picture this: After an aggressive promotion that resulted in close to two thousand downloads, I proudly unveil my email subscriber list, and you won't believe the thunderous applause—it's got a whopping two members! Yes, you heard that right. Two. Not two hundred, not twenty-two. Just two lone souls who, bless their hearts, probably subscribed by accident while chasing an online coupon for catnip.

So, dear readers, with little left in my wallet and my hopes shattered, I was on the verge of giving up. But don't worry! This story has only just begun. Listen in as I gather my wits, don my armor, and jump on the unpredictable roller coaster that is self-publishing. Because if there's one thing we've learned, it's that success requires a level of tenacity that rivals a cat in its pursuit of that moving red dot.

If there's one thing we've learned, it's that success requires a level of tenacity that rivals a cat in its pursuit of that moving red dot.

On a gloomy day, overnight rain painted the ground outside, leaving it wet and forlorn. Peering through the living room window, I spotted my beloved cat, Floofy, crouched beneath a tree, fixated on a group of distant birds. Her eyes were locked on those feathered early birds, her tail swaying in perfect rhythm. Ah, the classic hunting posture! Floofy was ready to embark on her favorite activity—hunting.

Since her first birthday, Floofy has brought home an assortment of prey. Birds of all sizes, alive or not, mice, lizards—you name it. I've scolded her countless times, reminding her that birds are friends, not prey. I used to scatter bird feed in the front yard, but I've stopped doing that out of fear that it would become a sugary death trap luring our feathered friends into Floofy's clutches. I even attached a bell to Floofy's collar to warn the birds. It has proven to be effective, and her successful hunts have significantly decreased. I feel a twinge of guilt for tampering with Floofy's feline dignity, but I know it's for the greater good—to protect the vulnerable.

Driven by curiosity and mentally exhausted from my "war room" (a.k.a. my study), I decided to observe Floofy while sipping my morning coffee. There she sat, patient as a saint. Utterly still and silent. It struck me that her fur color was a masterful camouflage, seamlessly blending with her surroundings. When a bird drew near, Floofy pounced! Startled, I let out a yelp, spilling coffee on the uncarpeted floor. Fortunately, Floofy missed her target, and the bird fled for safety. Floofy made a few more attempts before calling it a day. She strolled back indoors, brushed against my lower leg, and meowed a cheerful "good morning." Just another day in the life of a cat.

After serving Floofy her breakfast and tidying up the spilled coffee, I found myself seated next to a contented cat, blissfully grooming her fur. I turned to Floofy and posed a weighty question: "Should I quit self-publishing?" Floofy ceased her grooming, locking her wise green eyes onto mine. Her facial expression seemed to say, "Quit? I just did, momentarily. I'll strike again tomorrow." Oh! I felt like I was being hit by a stick on my head. I received an astonished wake-up call. It is not about quitting. All I needed was a break.

We all need a breather now and then, just like a marathon runner who stops for a cup of lemonade. It's just a pit stop to refuel our engines! A break is always beneficial when one feels stuck, low on energy, or tight on resources. We are humans. We all have ups and downs. When we are stuck, we should allow ourselves to take a break. The path to success is a long one. We need to allow ourselves time to learn from the experience and recharge our energy, then strike again when our battery is recharged.

It suddenly dawned on me why I had felt defeated. I hadn't given myself time to reset. I thought I was being persistent, but persisting in the wrong direction only depleted my energy and allowed the sense of defeat to grow stronger. Worst of all, I neglected to replenish my resources. Lost in thought, I expressed my gratitude by scratching Floofy's sweet spot—a tender spot on her lower neck that she adores. Purring with satisfaction, she taught me the importance of finding joy in simple pleasures.

I made my way to the study, where I diffused the calming aroma of sandalwood. The scent filled the room, soothing my weary mind. Returning to the living room, I noticed Floofy preparing for a nap. Before she drifted off to dreamland, I posed a question to Floofy. "Would you like to co-author our next book?" Squinting her eyes and appearing puzzled, she blinked slowly, then rolled over, exposing her belly. Ah, the age-old trap! Beware, for touching her belly means inviting scratches or bites. However, her gesture conveyed happiness. To me, that meant consent. I therefore followed with my second question, "shall we do a high-content or low-content book?" She remained silent, so I repeated the question.

My daughter, overhearing our conversation, I meant my monologue, shouted from her bedroom, "Mom, who are you talking to?" I replied, "I'm asking Floofy if we should do a high-content or low-content book together." My daughter chimed in, "Floofy's a cat, Mom! Of course, she needs high protein." Ah, perfect! It was settled. Floofy and I would create a high-content book together. This is the story behind our collaboration—a harmonious partnership between a human and her beloved feline co-author.

Quit? I just did. I will pounce again tomorrow!

Bonus Page

Wait a minute! Before we dive back into this delightful adventure, Floofy and I have a special invitation for you. Picture this: Floofy gazes at you with her clear green eyes, meowing, "You're invited!"

As a token of our eternal gratitude for joining us on this literary escapade, I present to you a marvelous bonus—a companion book that's as enchanting as Floofy herself! This delightful short read is filled with captivating photos, capturing those priceless moments we've shared throughout these stories. Oh, but there's more! Flip through the pages and discover Floofy's philosophical meows, brimming with wisdom and whimsy. And uncover some never-before-told tales that will tickle your funny bone and warm your heart.

Obtaining this treasured gem is as easy as giving Floofy a gentle head scratch. All we ask is a tiny favor—a moment of your time to hit that marvelous subscribe link below. By joining our esteemed email list, you'll gain access to this extraordinary book, absolutely FREE! Floofy's adorable face and literary treasures, all at your fingertips.

So, my dear friend, seize this opportunity to immerse yourself in Floofy's world like never before. Subscribe, and let us whisk you away on a journey filled with laughter, enlightenment, and a touch of   feline magic. Together, we shall conquer the literary landscape, one meow at a time!

Grab your copy by scanning the QR code or visiting here:

https://soulspress.com/opt-in-page-cats-wisdom

Chapter 2
Defining Your Unique Proposition

"I couldn't care less about those who turn up their noses at me. I embrace my own brand of uniqueness, and I draw in those who appreciate me for who I am."

Floofy, The Unapologetically Unique Feline

An Introduction to Floofy

Allow me to introduce you to the enigmatic and mischievous Floofy. With a heart as delicate as a butterfly's wing, she holds a faintness towards strangers, especially those small humans. The moment visitors step foot into our abode, Floofy becomes the Houdini of the feline world, vanishing into thin air or swiftly making her exit through the cat door. Poof! Gone in a flash!

A chair kick or the tiniest noise can send her sprinting like she's training for the Cat Olympics. It's like a game of "Catch Floofy if You Can." But here's the antilogy—the vacuum cleaner seems to hold no power over her. Nope, she'll just stay chill nearby, completely unbothered, as if she's basking in the white noise symphony of cleanliness. Go figure!

Cuddling? Not in Floofy's playbook, my friend. She's got her own agenda—a masterclass in independence. Yet, within those independent vibes lies the secret sauce of our connection. It's when she decides to curl up beside me on the sofa or claim her cozy spot near my feet on those frosty winter nights that I know I've earned the Floofy seal of approval. It's a rare and cherished privilege.

Feeding time is the moment Floofy unveils her true genius. With impeccable timing and a relentless spirit, she never fails to remind me, down to the second, that her delicate tummy requires sustenance. But here's the twist—she's a sly one. Oh yes, she plays the "Did I Eat or Didn't I?" game like a seasoned pro. Is it a genuine case of forgetfulness or a clever ruse to secure extra treats from my unsuspecting hands? Only Floofy knows the answer to that puzzling riddle.

In our household, I am Floofy's favorite human, followed closely by my daughter. My husband, well, let's just say Floofy is an opportunist. When I'm away, venturing overseas or otherwise absent, she shamelessly turns to him for her culinary needs. It seems her mischievous side amplifies when I'm around, an undeniable testament to our unique connection.

So, brace yourself for the unpredictable whirlwind of Floofy's world—a feline full of surprises, mischief, and undying loyalty. She keeps us on our toes, forever reminding us that laughter, companionship, and a touch of craziness can be found in the most captivating and mysterious creatures. Prepare for the purrfectly unpredictable adventure ahead!

Finding Your Unique Proposition

There is a school bus pick-up/ drop-off point near my house. Near the school bus stop, just around 3:30 p.m. each day, a plump orange cat would sit near a lamppost, eagerly awaiting the arrival of passersby. Initially, I assumed this feline was dutifully awaiting the return of a beloved young master from the school bus. However, upon closer observation, I discovered the truth. This charming orange fellow simply sought the affectionate pats and adoration from the cat-loving kids passing by. Oh, how heartwarming! It made me ponder the stark contrast to my mischievous Floofy. Children, you see, happen to be her sworn nemeses, capable of sending her soul fleeing from her very body. Does this imply that Mr. Orange is more favored than Miss Floofy?

As this whimsical encounter danced within my thoughts, a distant memory resurfaced—a recollection from the day I embraced Floofy as a treasured addition to my family, plucked from the shelter of the SPCA. In that bustling atmosphere, dozens of cats awaited their forever homes, each whispering tales of longing and hope. Overhearing snippets of conversations, I glimpsed into the hearts of potential adopters, their words spinning a tapestry of empathy and compassion:

"Look at this sweetie, so gentle and quiet. Mom, can we take her home?"

"Oh, an adult cat? Poor thing, nobody will want it. But I'll take you in. I'll love you, don't feel sad."

Woman: "Why does this cat only have one eye?"

Staff: "Oh, that's a defect. The other eye had a severe infection, and the vet had to remove it. The cat will always have just one eye."

Woman: "That's heartbreaking. Let me take this cat, or else no one else will."

These tender exchanges unveiled the essence of finding one's unique value proposition. In the realm of feline companionship, just as in the realm of our written endeavors, it is not a matter of being favored by all, nor is it a race to outshine our peers. Rather, it is about embracing our individuality and the distinctive qualities that make us who we are. It is in recognizing the beauty of our own proposition that we find our rightful place within the hearts of those who resonate with our essence.

So, dear writer, take a moment to reflect upon your own unique value proposition. Just as Mr. Orange found his calling among the cat-loving children, and Floofy reigns supreme in her mischievous glory, it is through embracing our individuality that we carve a path of connection and resonance. As we venture forth into the vast realms of creativity, let's not be a cat who meows at everyone, but about captivating the hearts of those who truly appreciate and cherish what we have to offer. A successful author must possess their own distinctive proposition and remain fiercely loyal to it.

> A successful author must possess their own distinctive proposition and remain fiercely loyal to it.

Embracing the Company of Those You Can Delight

Once I made the decision to realign my self-publishing strategy and reignite my passion, the time came to ponder on the all-important question: What should my next book be about, in other words, what book should I create? As Floofy had been my faithful companion throughout the self-publishing training, and we've watched countless YouTube videos together, I couldn't help but believe she must have possessed an abundance of knowledge on the subject, just like me........I mean enough knowledge....okay? So, naturally, I decided to extend an invitation for a discussion.

Calling out Floofy's name, I eagerly awaited her presence. Yet there was no sign of her in the house. Peering out the window, I discovered her basking in the sun on the driveway. There she sat, like a diligent guard dog stationed in front of the garage. I called her, but her reaction? Non-existent. Not even the slightest twitch of her whiskers. Determined to seek her input, I approached her, knelt down, and gently scratched her neck. Employing my most soothing and inviting voice, I asked, "Hey, darling, what do you think we should write for our book?" In response, Floofy merely shifted her posture, rolling onto her side without uttering a meow.

At that moment, a lady walking her white Poodle strolled by. She cast a smile and nodded in Floofy's direction, exclaiming, "Look at the cute cat, isn't she adorable?" Floofy remained silent. I smiled back at the lady while patiently awaiting Floofy's guidance. Then, two teenage girls passed by. The taller girl turned to her companion, possibly her sister, and murmured, "Hey, look at that patchy creature. Is that even a cat?" Oh, the audacity! She muttered it under her breath, and I pretended not to hear the impolite comment.

Yet, Floofy remained unperturbed by the girls' remarks. She continued to revel in my company and the affectionate strokes of my hand. To Floofy, the sun still bathed her in warmth, and her human remained caring. The world hadn't changed for her; she was still the mischievous and beloved feline of our household. She knew she would always receive the love of her beloved owner, and most importantly, her meals for the day. Why would she concern herself with the opinions of others?

Ah, the epiphany strikes with delightful clarity! The question is not about "what", but "who"? Not about "what book to create", but "who are our target readers?" We need to focus on the right people, and not to be distracted by noise.

In my ventures of yore, I found myself overly consumed by the labyrinth of keyword research, the pursuit of profitable niches, and the never-ending quest to produce books that sell like hotcakes.

Oh, how I have conveniently forgotten about the true essence of it all—my readers! Who are these marvelous individuals I yearn to forge connections with? What sparks their interest in my books?

Certainly, we must not underestimate the importance of crafting a stellar book. Yes, that remains a vital piece of the puzzle! However, no matter how exceptional your book may be, you must also have the uncanny ability to connect with your readers. Those who like you. Yes, indeed! It matters not if you possess a brilliant idea, a treasure trove of keywords, or a niche that promises bountiful rewards. For in the midst of this literary realm, a fierce battleground awaits.

You see, as we traverse this ever-expanding universe of authors, equipped with the same arsenal of research tools and wielding similar techniques, we find ourselves faced with a sea of competition. Cue the dramatic music...... When all is said and done, and everyone strives to produce impeccably researched and professionally written books, complete with magnificent covers created by the most talented of designers, we reach a crossroads—a point where differentiation becomes a distant dream. It is at this juncture that the key to success lies within those who truly comprehend their customers, who build genuine relationships, and who strike a harmonious chord that resonates with their cherished readers.

So, my fellow scribes, let us venture forth with the knowledge that it is not solely about delivering a fantastic book—though that undoubtedly holds its merit. Nay, it is about unveiling a world that captures the hearts and minds of our readers. It is about understanding their desires, their hopes, and their dreams. For amidst the clamor of competitors who strive for excellence, it is those who forge deep connections, who understand their readers' very souls, and who create an unparalleled symphony of resonance that shall flourish in this extraordinary realm of literature.

Also, we need to remember that not everyone will be a fan. Oh no, there will always be those who raise their eyebrows and shake their heads disapprovingly. But our focus should never waver. Our mission is to craft books that speak to those who genuinely appreciate and resonate with our words. We must strive to please those who can be pleased. As for those who cannot be pleased, well, let them do their grumpy dance elsewhere. We shall not let their disapproval dampen our spirits. Onward we go, my friends, pen in hand and laughter in our hearts!

"Meow……" As I was pounding away at the keyboard, riding the tsunami of my brilliant ideas, I heard the creaky door of my study slowly swing open, like a reluctant participant in a cheesy horror movie. Floofy stood there; her meow signaled a sense of urgency. I knew it was dinner time.

> Strive to please those who can be pleased. We shall not let disapprovals dampen our spirits.

Sharpening Your Senses

Floofy, like all felines, possesses an insatiable curiosity that knows no bounds. From the moment she entered my home, her inquisitive nature has taken the spotlight. I eagerly purchased a plethora of fancy cat toys, relishing in the anticipation of watching her play. Little did I know, Floofy had her own mischievous agenda. She would deconstruct these expensive playthings, dismantling them with a fervor that left me in awe. Take, for instance, the perplexing ball-in-tube toy. Its purpose was to guide the balls around an eight-shaped track, but Floofy had her own interpretations, ingeniously retrieving the balls in ways that defied logic. Who needs instruction manuals when you have a cat's unwavering creativity? Oops….I almost forgot that cats don't read manuals.

Like many cat owners, I quickly learned that no matter how much I splurged on fancy toys, they couldn't hold a candle to the simple pleasures found right within our humble abode. The once pristine scratching post? It might as well have been a piece of modern art, untouched and gathering dust. The majestic cat tree, designed for climbing and exploring? It stood there in all its glory, perpetually vacant, while Floofy found her true sanctuary perched upon the keyboard of my laptop. And as for cat tunnels? They might as well have been invisible, while a lowly plastic bag became the epitome of her feline fascination. Yes, I'm aware it's labeled "not a toy, keep away from children!"—but try telling that to Floofy, who couldn't resist its mesmerizing allure. Who knew the greatest feline joy could be found in the simplest of household objects?

Today, as I toiled away in my study, a cacophony of sounds erupted outside. It seemed as though Floofy was engaged in a ferocious battle. My heart skipped a beat, fearing she had encountered another living creature or, heaven forbid, something that used to be alive. I ventured outside cautiously, only to discover her dueling with a black wire cable tie. The origin of this peculiar plaything remained a mystery, but Floofy reveled in its simple delight. With twists, rolls, pounces, and jumps, she transformed the most ordinary object into a game filled with excitement and joy.

Once again, I found myself reflecting on the wisdom of our feline companions. Isn't this a strength every writer should possess? The ability to infuse creativity into every subject, to uncover the extraordinary within the mundane. A cat teaches us that even the simplest, most unremarkable aspects of life can be woven into a tapestry of vibrant colors, whimsical tales, and captivating narratives. So, my writer friends, let us embrace Floofy's curious cat-titude and unlock the magic of turning the ordinary into the extraordinary.

Even the simplest, most unremarkable aspects of life can be woven into a tapestry of vibrant colors, whimsical tales, and captivating narratives.

Chapter 3
Navigate Your Own Route

"*I may not always know the exact route, but I trust that the journey itself will guide me to where I need to be.*"

Floofy - The Tireless Explorer

Finding Your Unique Route

Not long ago, I discovered Floofy perched on the rooftop, defying all odds. I couldn't fathom how she managed to reach such heights with no apparent safe path. As visions of firefighters rescuing stranded kittens danced in my head, I contemplated the embarrassment of calling for help—either a dim-witted cat or a neglectful owner, they might think!

With keen observation, I studied Floofy's rooftop rendezvous, determined to unravel her secret. And there it was, amidst the backdrop of nature's verdant embrace: an overgrown tree, its branches reaching out like a welcoming hand to our humble garden shed. A hidden gateway to the skies above, it beckoned Floofy to embark on her lofty adventure. With a sprightly hop from the fence, a graceful leap onto the shed roof, and a triumphant tail flick, she had forged her own path to the summit. I reckoned it wasn't a meticulously planned expedition, mind you—I believed she stumbled upon this lofty adventure while exploring her surroundings.

As fate would have it, my husband decided to trim down the overgrown tree before summer bid farewell. To my disbelief, a week later, I found Floofy atop the roof again. How was this even possible? There was no longer anything connecting to the house. Intrigued and dropping everything else, I embarked on a mission to solve the mystery. An hour slipped away. The rustling of leaves provided a gentle symphony, punctuated by the occasional chirping of birds. Stubborn as ever, Floofy remained perched on her lofty throne, her eyes gleaming with a playful secret, as if to taunt, "I'll never reveal my secret route." Just as I was about to give up, my daughter's urgent cry pierced the air, "Mom, your phone is ringing!" Reluctantly tearing my gaze away from the rooftop marvel, I went into the house and attended to the call. Upon my return, I witnessed Ms. Mischief strolling inside the house with a mischievous smile played upon her whiskers, as if to say, "Haha, I've outsmarted you again!"

Through my self-publishing journey, I've encountered countless tales of success. Reflecting upon their achievements, I pondered the elusive ingredient that set them apart. Was there a magical formula they all possessed? Inspired by my furry friend's wisdom, a metaphorical light bulb illuminated within me. Suddenly, I thought I had cracked it! The common factor was their unwavering determination to find their own route, just like Floofy discovering her path to the rooftop. To others, it may seem impossible, but for those with indomitable persistence and the willingness to pave their own way, success awaits.

Taking Floofy's rooftop adventure as a case study, it's clear that there's more than one route to the destination. In fact, there are multiple destinations, and each of us has our own unique pursuits. Your journey is not mine, and each destination boasts countless paths leading to the same goal. If we were to tackle this as a math problem, the possibilities would be infinite, with numerous correct answers.

May this insight inspire you on your own path. There's no one-size-fits-all formula for success. Each of us must embark on the exhilarating quest of finding our personal route to the rooftop. We must concoct our own secret recipe for success, embracing our uniqueness and differentiation. Once you've unlocked it, you're destined for greatness. While it may not necessarily guarantee wealth in the realm of self-publishing, the immeasurable satisfaction and fulfillment of being a recognized writer are priceless rewards indeed.

For those with indomitable persistence and the willingness to pave their own way, success awaits.

Embracing Setbacks with a Roaring Cat-titude

Today, I'm taking advantage of the nice weather by doing some gardening. I must agree with you. This is really unusual, as I normally avoid situations where I might be exposed to too much sunlight due to the risk of sunburn. And if it seems too cloudy, you know it could start raining at any moment. To top it all off, the wind is too strong. No way out, and of course it was raining, the worst possible combination. Well, I guess I've learned that there's really no such thing as a good time to plant....I hope you feel like you have a better grasp of who I am now.

I was cleaning up the flower bed and pulling weeds from the edge of the driveway. Then I heard a huge crash behind me, like though something had fallen from a tree. When I turned around, I noticed a shattered branch lying on the ground. It was roughly as long as my arm from shoulder to palm, and it had a stem and some leafy offshoots. My eyes couldn't adjust to the sunlight. It took me all of two seconds to notice Floofy among the shattered branches. She was in fact the key contributor to the loud noise. Quickly trying to piece together what had happened, I reasoned that she must have stepped on some weakened branches that had collapsed under her weight. Although I could not witness her landing posture, I am told that cats always land gracefully on their feet. I supposed Floofy shouldn't be any adversely special. It wasn't supposed to be her lucky day, but the branches and Floofy landed on the grass instead of the concrete driveway. Thank God for my cat!

The story took an intriguing turn. Floofy, with her morning meow and graceful cat strut, approached me as if nothing had happened. Oh, the thick-skinned fluffball tried to pull a fast one on me, but that slight glimmer of embarrassment in her eyes gave her away. Nice try, Floofy! I couldn't help but smile. I reassured her with a tender stroke on her back, silently appreciating her unscathed state.

As I resumed my outdoor duties, Floofy's nonchalant reaction after the fall kept playing on my mind. It's truly remarkable how cats master the art of shrugging off setbacks. They approach difficulties with an air of "I meant to do that" or a casual "Who cares?" cat-titude. It's as if they're saying, "Falls happen. Life's full of surprises. Let's get back up and conquer that tree!"

And speaking of conquering, just ten minutes later, there she was, climbing the tree again. The fall hadn't left a single bad memory. Floofy's persistence was nothing short of astounding. It got me thinking about the valuable lesson we can learn from feline perseverance, especially in the unpredictable world of self-publishing.

In this journey of ups and downs, we need to channel our inner Floofy and cultivate the cat-titude of unwavering determination. When friends and family bombard us with questions like "How many books did you sell?" or "Are you making any money?" or even the classic "Why are you still doing this?"—we must hold our ground. Self-publishing is a unique path, and not everyone will understand it.

We need that undying cat-titude to sustain us through the disappointment, to push us forward when the market seems saturated, and doubts start to creep in. It's about standing tall on our own feet and forging ahead, knowing that setbacks are simply part of the deal. The more obstacles we encounter, the closer we are to success. It's all a matter of developing a success mindset—a belief in ourselves and the power of our subconscious.

I'm not one for mindfulness or meditation, but I firmly believe in the incredible power of our minds. In fact, my book "Unlock Success Mindset for Young Adults in 8 Days" examines deep into nurturing and developing the right mindset.

My friends! When sticky circumstances arise, remember to harness your inner cat. Embrace the setbacks as part of the journey to greatness. With the unwavering determination of a cat and the resilience to shrug it off, we can conquer any challenge that comes our way. Let's pounce on our dreams, chase success with wild abandon, and always keep a playful twinkle in our eyes.

With the unwavering determination of a cat and the resilience to shrug it off, we can conquer any challenge that comes our way.

Sustaining the Everlasting Curiosity

A very important meeting took place last week. I spent weeks getting ready, endless hours researching, and countless more hours practicing my scripts until I could recite them in my sleep. Where did this historic event take place? Zoom, of course, is none other than a fantastical digital realm. Working from home has many perks. Isn't it fantastic?

Now, in hindsight, I probably should have shut the door to my study. But hey, I was the only person home, and I've never had a feline gatecrasher before, so I took it all in stride. Little did I know that my trusty sidekick, Floofy, had a starring role to play in this high-stakes drama.

As I began my presentation, confidently showcasing my brilliance, Floofy decided it was the perfect time to make her grand entrance. With the camera on my laptop only capturing the top half of my body, she saw her chance to claim the prime real estate behind me—the gap between my back and the chair. And so, she gracefully leaped onto the seat, her presence hidden from the unsuspecting audience.

In a desperate attempt to maintain my professional composure, I discreetly contorted my left arm behind me, attempting to nudge her off the chair while still delivering my impeccable pitch. But the mischievous Floofy had other plans. Curiosity got the better of her. Perhaps she wondered why I was so enamored with this rectangular, shiny object or why my attention wasn't solely focused on her majestic presence.

With paws planted firmly on my back, she stood on two feet and peered over my left shoulder, her inquisitive gaze meeting mine. I couldn't help but let out a stifled yelp, hoping against hope that my audience hadn't noticed this unexpected addition to our virtual gathering. Were they too engrossed in the dazzling presentation slides I shared, or had they caught a glimpse of the feline intruder? The answer eluded me, and quite frankly, I wasn't eager to find out.

But you know what? This bizarre encounter got me thinking. Cats, with their fearless nature, remind us mere mortals of the importance of taking risks and embracing the unknown. Whether it's photobombing your Zoom calls or infiltrating the bathroom to uncover your secrets, these furry adventurers know a thing or two about stepping out of their comfort zones.

And guess what? We, humans, can learn from their audacious curiosity. Self-publishing, my friends, is a journey of exploration and self-discovery, not so different from a cat's wild escapades. It's about being brave enough to try new things, venturing into uncharted territories, and never assuming you have all the answers.

It's about channeling your passion and fearlessly exploring the realms of creativity and science.

Now, some naysayers might argue that cats don't understand the consequences of their actions. And to them, I say, "Precisely!" When you're in the early stages of the self-publishing process, like conducting keyword research, designing book covers, or outlining your masterpiece, it's time to unleash your inner cat. Be curious, my friends. Don't let the fear of consequences stifle your imagination; instead, venture out into the wider seas of possibilities.

Curiosity is key to unlocking your latent strengths too. It's about pushing your own boundaries, stepping into uncharted territories, and embracing the unknown like a true explorer. Who knows? You might discover hidden talents you never knew existed. The potential for greatness knows no bounds. So, summon your inner adventurer and boldly go where no one has gone before.

And remember, just like Floofy's unexpected cameo, the unexpected can often lead to the most memorable and extraordinary moments. So, don't be afraid, smile!

As you navigate the labyrinthine world of publishing, be open to new possibilities and uncharted territories. Let your imagination roam freely, unbounded by limitations. Just like a cat curiously paws at the unknown, dare to explore genres outside your comfort zone, experiment with fresh writing styles, and challenge conventional norms. Surprise yourself with the heights you can reach.

And when doubts creep in, as they often do, embrace that unwavering belief in your own abilities, that unshakeable confidence that says, "I can conquer the publishing world." Trust your unique voice, your storytelling prowess, and let your words dance upon the page with feline grace.

So, my friend, as you embark on your self-publishing odyssey, remember the lessons of our fearless feline companions. Be bold, be curious, and embrace the unknown with a mischievous glint in your eye. Take risks, savor the journey, and may your stories ignite the hearts and minds of readers far and wide.

Be bold, be curious, and embrace the unknown with a mischievous glint in your eye.

Nurturing Your Cat-Like Resilience

The old saying goes that cats have nine lives. I mean, seriously, have you witnessed their death-defying acrobatics? It's as if they have a secret stash of extra lives tucked away somewhere.

Worried about Floofy being picked on by older cats, we kept her indoors until her first birthday. Before that, a gray and white cat would frequently visit and roam around our house. One fateful night, my husband heard a loud crash, like something plummeting from the sky, only to discover Mr. Gray standing bewildered on our wooden deck just outside the living room. We chuckled, imagining he had dozed off on our roof, missed the sunset, and misjudged his landing. We offered him some cat food and a bowl of water. Miraculously, he seemed unscathed, enjoying a meal before finding his way back home. Talk about a lucky escape!

Observing cats fearlessly venture into the unknown, I've witnessed Floofy nibbling on power cords as a mischievous kitten. She once got herself entangled in my curtain veil, hanging mid-air like a feline acrobat, before gracefully descending with the veil in tatters. I can't help but wonder, are they curious because they know they're resilient, or are they resilient because their curiosity drives them to take risks? Could it be their ancient ancestors, the daredevils of the feline world, who passed down this curiosity through generations?

MY CAT BECOMES A SELF-PUBLISHER 51

The spiral of curiosity and resilience growing stronger with each new cat. Alas, I'm no zoologist, so the mysteries of feline evolution remain for the experts to unravel.

One thing is certain, though—Floofy isn't keen on squandering her nine lives on unnecessary risks. The sound of an approaching car engine or a barking dog can send her scurrying back home in a heartbeat. Yet, she's oblivious to the perils of lying smack dab in the middle of the driveway, eagerly welcoming me home. Picture this: I pull up, waiting for the garage door to open, when out of thin air, Floofy appears, plopping herself right in front of the car, rolling over and exposing her belly. She's the purrfect greeter, and I've become so trained that I always approach with caution, fearful of any cat-astrophic accidents.

Cats are the aristocracy of inquisitiveness, which is precisely why they benefit from having more than one shot at life. They're the daredevils of the animal kingdom, perpetually on the prowl, eager to discover and get themselves into all sorts of mischief. Without their resilience, their unquenchable curiosity could have spelled doom for their entire species. But no, they evolved incredible resistance to extinction, flourishing instead.

The cat's wisdom for self-publishing reveals a valuable lesson: to succeed in this ever-changing realm, one must embody the resilience of a cat. Self-publishing is a volatile journey where the market charges forward, customers evolve, preferences shift, and the rules of the game constantly change. Setbacks become a repetitive companion on this path. But fear not, for it is through unwavering resilience that you can outlive the competition and thrive. Just like the ancient cats with their nine lives, those who possess a high level of resilience can expand their influence, their bloodline in the publishing world.

I encourage you to cultivate a rubber-band resilience as you venture forth into the world of self-publishing. May your journey be filled with joy, fun, and perhaps a few delightful detours fueled by the catnip of creativity. In the realm of self-publishing, where rules shift like a cat's whims, and competition prowls relentlessly, tap into your inner feline spirit. Remember, setbacks are simply part of the grand adventure toward success. May your journey be marked with determination, perseverance, and the ability to adapt to the ever-changing landscape. Meow your way to success!

MY CAT BECOMES A SELF-PUBLISHER

The path to discovering your strengths involves a sense of curiosity and a willingness to explore various interests and experiences.

Chapter 4

Finding Your Purr-Suit

"Patience is not merely the ability to wait, but the purrfect art of embracing the present moment with a calm and observant mind."

Floofy – The Feline Zen

Embracing Patience and Observance

Today the surveillance camera at the front of my house seemed to be malfunctioning. As I reviewed the camera footage, something extraordinary caught my eye. The camera seemed to be working just fine, but the real star of the show was none other than Floofy herself. There she was, stealthily prowling, on a mission of utmost importance. Now, I couldn't see exactly what had captured her attention—a mischievous butterfly or a wriggling earthworm—but one thing was clear: Floofy was in her element. With a level of focus and patience that would put a Zen master to shame, she embraced her inner detective.

Watching Floofy in action made me stop and wonder. When was the last time I dedicated myself so fully to an activity? When did I last take a moment to savor my surroundings, using all my senses to absorb the stories and inspiration they had to offer? Why does time always feel like it's slipping through my fingers, as if every moment must be spent on a quest for productivity?

In my pur-rsuit of self-publishing knowledge, I've immersed myself in countless YouTube videos where successful entrepreneurs extol the virtues of patience. But what does it truly mean? Upon careful reflection, I realized I had been "patient" in a hurry. Always racing to the finish line, trying to speed up the journey to success, as if I could teleport my way to multiple six-figure results. But is the dollar sign the real destination or just a shiny target? Have I lost sight of the delightful twists and turns along the way?

Even if a self-publishing guru needs a solid twelve months to launch his second KDP account into the stratosphere, why on earth did I ever think I could do it in half the time? If I'm fixated solely on the endgame, I might miss out on the whimsical, marvelous moments that make the journey truly worthwhile. Is the experience of being a self-publisher not equally important as a pile of dollar bills? For me, the answer is a resounding meow. Sure, a few extra thousand dollars might give me a sense of accomplishment, plus financial wellness, okay! I am not pretending. But it's the laughter, growth, and unexpected adventures that would bring true fulfillment. What do you think?

I'm absolutely pawsitive that many of you can relate. Self-publishing requires two essential ingredients: time and, let's face it, a pinch of insanity. But above all, it's not about making a quick buck. It's about embracing your aspirations, nurturing your passions, and embarking on a quirky journey of entrepreneurship.

Returning to our feline guru, Floofy, her patient and observant nature is simply part of her feline DNA. Cats, those cunning hunters, have an uncanny ability to focus and wait, even when their tummies grumble. They know that by channeling their inner Zen master, their chances of pouncing triumphantly increase tenfold. It's a valuable lesson we humans can learn—no, scratch that—we can embrace, reminding us to approach life's challenges with a dash of curiosity, a sprinkle of patience, and an unwavering belief in the magic of the journey itself.

Approach life's challenges with a dash of curiosity, a sprinkle of patience, and an unwavering belief in the magic of the journey itself.

Retrieving Your Needle in the Haystack

Feeding time is when Floofy truly shines, showcasing her exceptional talent. I usually serve her a delightful blend of dry and wet cat food. Of course, like any feline connoisseur, Floofy adores the wet food. Sometimes, I even use it as a special treat. Her excitement is palpable as she watches me retrieve the supplies from the cupboard, accompanied by her cheerful meows and the sparkle in her eyes.

Lately, I stumbled upon something quite intriguing. Alright, I'll do what any decent storyteller would do and begin from the beginning. Floofy's favorite wet food comes in handy pouches, which are enough for two meals when mixed with the dry food. To preserve the remaining half, I fold over the top and secure it with a long tail clip. Curiously enough, whenever I retrieve the half-used pouch from the fridge and unfold it, Floofy magically materializes out of nowhere. It's as if a melodious tune made of foil pouch unfolding summons this mischievous marvel. In an instant, Floofy sits before me, striking her most picture-perfect pose.

Initially, I brushed it off as mere coincidence. Yet, it soon became a regular occurrence. Every time I folded or unfolded that aluminum foil pouch, Floofy would appear. I tested it with various container bags, including plastic ones and other food wraps, but to no avail.

Floofy possesses a unique ability—the uncanny discernment to recognize the sound of her beloved treat. It's akin to her magical aptitude for finding a needle in a haystack.

Contemplating this phenomenon, I couldn't help but wish for a similar discerning ability to identify profitable topics or keywords for self-publishing. I yearned to filter out the noise and distractions, focusing solely on the profitable niche. How does one distinguish a good topic from a less promising one? How can we uncover hidden gold mines amidst the vast ocean of possibilities?

I've watched countless YouTube videos and repeatedly rewatched training materials provided by my instructor. I'm almost certain that no top-kept secrets are being withheld by these gurus. They don't possess a success formula exclusive to them, yet they've become experts and amassed fortunes through their books, leaving us in awe and, perhaps, a tad jealous. So, what exactly is the secret sauce to self-publishing success?

As I observed Floofy relishing her meal, I murmured my thoughts aloud, noticing her ears attentively moving as I spoke. Even while eating, she remained aware of her surroundings.

Blink! I had an epiphany. Floofy's ability to discern the sound was learned, not innate. While cats naturally possess excellent hearing, differentiating sounds that lead to pleasure is a skill acquired through persistent and consistent attention to their favorite activity.

In the realm of self-publishing, those with the strongest instincts have honed their skills through long-term learning, adaptation, and experimentation. Genius may exist, but even geniuses and world-class athletes require training, coaching, and repetitive reinforcement to become gold medalists, much like Olympic athletes.

It's true that some individuals achieve thousands or even five-figure incomes with their first book, but such luck is impossible to replicate. Instead, I prefer dedicating my time to perfecting my craft rather than attempting to comprehend why some people appear luckier than others. Methods and practices can be learned and trained, but luck remains elusive, much like a fairytale. How often do we witness couples falling in love at first sight and living happily ever after?

Alright! You're probably wondering how we can train ourselves to expertly find needles in haystacks. My belief is to learn from the pros. I suggest reading and studying bestsellers and top-selling books from indie publishers. Learn from the success stories of others. While replicating someone else's success may be challenging, immersing ourselves in their works allows us to develop a discerning taste for what's good and what's not. This ability is invaluable, similar to visiting your competitors' restaurants before opening your own, understanding each other's competitive edges within the landscape.

What we learn from self-publishing instructors provides essential knowledge. These skills enable us to start on the right foot, saving valuable time, energy, and money that would otherwise be wasted in convoluted mazes. However, these basic skills cannot guarantee success. Each of us must strive to perfect our own crafts. This is what our respected instructors cannot explicitly reveal, as we are all unique individuals. It's not that they want to keep these secrets from us.

Wow, Floofy! You wise little cat. Your wisdom is truly mind-blowing. You effortlessly unveil these deep secrets, this mystical and hidden intelligence. You didn't need to employ hard-to-understand words. In fact, you didn't utter a single meow. You didn't even need to twitch your whiskers or paw me an essay. Your wisdom revealed itself through the subtle movement of your ears and the glimmer in your eyes. How can I adequately express my gratitude?

I generously spooned some more wet food treats into her bowl, and Floofy appeared puzzled, wondering how she had earned an extra supply of her favorite delicacy. She locked her gaze with mine, seeking reassurance. I nodded, signaling my approval. With that, she happily resumed savoring her delightful meal.

I prefer dedicating my time to perfecting my craft rather than attempting to comprehend why some people appear luckier than others.

Cultivating an Invaluable Relationship with Readers

I must admit, it was my daughter who insisted on adopting Floofy from the SPCA. Initially, I was skeptical. Floofy's appearance didn't fit my preconceived notions of what a cat should look like. Since childhood, I had envisioned cats with tabby patterns or ginger-colored fur. I never expected a cat that resembled spilled ink. It seemed as though God had run out of spare parts while crafting her, hastily assembling different components before calling it a day. My daughter persisted and even named our new feline companion "Floofy"—a name whose meaning eluded me.

However, once Floofy arrived and became a part of our family, I gradually fell in love with her. It was like applying thin coats of nail polish—one layer at a time, waiting for each coat to dry before applying another. Oops, sorry! I suppose not all readers use nail polish. What I mean is that building a relationship is akin to painting a wall—it cannot be rushed. It requires patience, commitment, and, of course, love, to achieve a satisfying end result.

After a year of Floofy being a part of our lives, she became an irreplaceable family member. We always considered her needs before making important decisions. When renovating the house, we opted for painted walls instead of wallpaper after Miss Mischievous shredded the corners. The ground floor carpet was replaced with laminated floors since Floofy had marked her territories, and even the most potent detergents couldn't eliminate the persistent odor. These incidents, among many other expensive and troublesome encounters, became cherished memories, all contributing to the growth of our love for her. This, I believe, is what a true relationship is all about—it cannot be measured in monetary terms, despite the occasional inconveniences... or rather, troubles.

Now, let me share a story. Last Christmas, as a reward for a significant decision I had made for my family and myself, I decided to treat myself to a massage chair. Those who know me personally are aware of what I'm referring to, but I won't elaborate on details here. After comparing prices, specifications, and driving to showrooms to test different models, I finally settled on a mid-range option—a balance between functionality and cost-effectiveness. I eagerly awaited its delivery, clearing a spot in the living room in anticipation of this long-awaited piece of furniture. I recalled the sheer joy I felt when the delivery was scheduled just one week before Christmas.

Finally, the massage chair arrived, and it blended seamlessly with its surroundings—the color harmonizing perfectly with the rest of the room. I was overjoyed, engrossed in reading the user manual and exploring its features. What an experience it was! The chair even had a seat-warming function. Imagine, sitting in a massage chair with the seat warming function turned on, watching your favorite TV show during the Christmas holidays.

The next morning, as I entered the living room, rage consumed me. Floofy had no intention of respecting my household authority. She had claimed the new chair as her own, marking it with her territory. Since the chair was made of synthetic leather, the liquid wasn't absorbed, leaving a visible puddle of yellow on the seat. I was livid.

After cleaning up the mess, I carried Floofy over to the chair, placing her face close to the spot she had soiled, and proceeded to give her a stern lecture. "Floofy, this is unacceptable. You have your own litter box, and you must never relieve yourself outside of it. Mommy is not pleased!" Floofy seemed to understand the gravity of my words, avoiding eye contact as guilt washed over her.

Did the story end there? Far from it. The conflict continued, and she remained determined to replace her litter box with my massage chair. This happened on three more occasions before I resorted to covering the chair with a piece of canvas I found in the garden shed. However, this only resulted in an unsightly living room. The color no longer matched, and the elegance of the furniture was obscured.

I turned to the internet in search of a solution, trying cat repellent spray, motion-activated vibration sirens, and canvas seat covers—I tried them all. Finally, I stumbled upon a cat-repellent scat mat that served its purpose. Just imagine the stress, time, and cost I invested in this endeavor.

So, what's the feline wisdom hidden in this tale that's relevant to self-publishing? It's the importance of nurturing a close relationship with our target readers. Such relationships take time to develop and don't happen overnight. They require effort, commitment, and a whole lot of love. Once the bond is established, you become an inseparable part of each other's lives, and your readers will stick around. Yes, we're all human, and we make mistakes from time to time. Yet, our relationship with our readers serves as a resilient bond. They'll be forgiving, understanding, and supportive even when we stumble.

Our relationship with our readers serves as a resilient bond. They'll be forgiving, understanding, and supportive even when we stumble.

Unveiling the Wisdom of Reader Bonding

Floofy waltzed into my life like a furry tornado, turning my cat obsession into a full-blown cat-astrophe of pet ownership. When I was small, my family used to have dogs as pets, but I have always wanted a cat. I've had my fair share of pets growing up, but my bond with Floofy was on a whole other level. And let me tell you, this bond became crystal clear during this one epic incident that is worth sharing.

It was a dreary, rainy day, with a persistent drizzle casting a melancholic atmosphere. Despite being an indoor cat before her first birthday, Floofy's curiosity about the outside world was insatiable, and she often sought opportunities to venture outside the house. One day, while I was away on a business trip, my husband called me in distress—Floofy had managed to escape, and their attempts to find her had been in vain. Panic and worry consumed me as I racked my brain for insights gained from my extensive research for cat knowledge. A glimmer of hope emerged—a flickering flame of knowledge that whispered, "She wouldn't stray far, as she seldom goes out and home is her sanctuary." I instructed my husband and daughter to thoroughly search our garden and backyard. An hour later, my husband called again, and relief washed over me when he shared that he had found Floofy hiding beneath the deck.

However, coaxing her back inside proved to be a challenge. Even her favorite treats failed to entice her.

Overwhelmed and unable to assist from afar, I anxiously awaited news from home. Later that night, good news arrived in the form of a WhatsApp message—a photo of Floofy comfortably grooming herself on the sofa. The story that unfolded left me awestruck. It was Floofy who had meowed at my daughter's bedroom window, seeking help to gain reentry into the house. It was obvious that her rumbling tummy had compelled her to find sustenance and prompted her to ask for assistance.

But it wasn't this incident that revealed our special bond. A month later, when I was at home, Floofy sneaked out again. I called out Floofy's name while standing outside the front door. The bell that was attached to her collar could be heard jingling from a considerable distance, and it was joined by her quick footstep as she ran gleefully towards me in delight. This was no mere coincidence. From that point forward, I discovered that she exclusively acknowledged my call. When others attempted to summon her, her ears would twitch, acknowledging the sound, but her response remained reserved—only with me did she show enthusiasm and an eagerness to engage.

Floofy had not only recognized my voice but also familiarized herself with my routine. She would patiently wait outside my bedroom each morning, eagerly greet me in the driveway upon my return home and appear at my study when she knew it was feeding time. Occupying a particular spot on the sofa, she would accompany me as we enjoyed television together. My husband, although a tad envious, marveled at Floofy's dog-like behavior when it came to our bond.

Cats are renowned for their independence, cherishing their own company and following their personal preferences. Thus, it is a true honor to have cultivated such an intimate relationship with Floofy—a free spirit in her own right. This unique connection made me realize the wisdom cats impart: our relationship with readers holds a similar significance. Others may have difficulty understanding the breadth of this connection because it is a complex tapestry made with intricate strands that cannot be replicated under any circumstances. Learning about our readers' preferences and opinions, being open to constructive criticism, and engaging with the issues that matter to them are the keys to building a loyal fan base. In this blend of fantasy and the enchantment of literature, we embark on a quest in which we learn that knowing and connecting with our readers is crucial to our success as writers. Once the bond is built, our readers will be longing for the next chapter of our literary adventure as we continue to uncover this mystery.

Learning about our readers' preferences and opinions, being open to constructive criticism, and engaging with the issues that matter to them are the keys to building a loyal fan base.

Chapter 5
Do It for Yourself and You Mean It

> "*The thrill is not in catching the red dot, but in chasing life's moving targets with whimsical delight. Happiness resides in the journey, not the destination.*"
>
> — Floofy, Chief Feline Adventurer

Doing It for Yourself

Today, I observed Floofy engaging in an almost obsessive grooming session. Concerned, I recalled those documentaries about animals developing anxiety and resorting to repetitive behaviors like parrots plucking their own feathers, dogs licking certain body parts bald, and cats incessantly licking their fur. I couldn't help but wonder what might have triggered Floofy's unusual behavior.

I retraced the events of the day, but nothing out of the ordinary came to mind. It was just another day. I woke up, enjoyed my morning coffee, and savored a piece of toast. I went about my grooming routine, meticulously attending to each detail before changing into my office attire—yes, even though I was working from home. Some may argue that dressing up for remote work is unnecessary, but I've always believed in maintaining professionalism. I've heard coworkers mentioned wearing pajama pants with a shirt and jacket, and the mental image alone brought a smile to my face. Oh, lost in thought again! I must return to reality. Floofy was still licking her fur.

Approaching Floofy, I gently stroked her back and inquired, "Darling, why the nonstop grooming today? Is everything alright?" She meowed in response, and there were no visible signs of distress. Her inexplicable behavior remained a mystery.

MY CAT BECOMES A SELF-PUBLISHER

During dinner, I shared Floofy's peculiar behavior with my daughter and husband. They turned to look at Floofy, who was washing her face after her supper before settling down to groom her fur once more. She seemed to pay extra attention to her back, contorting her neck at astonishing angles. I always found it mesmerizing how cats could achieve such flexibility. Floofy meticulously licked her fur, a sight I usually found delightful. However, today, it filled me with worry.

After finishing the dishes, I reached for my hand cream. My daughter's eyes caught sight of a new tube of expensive hand cream and she exclaimed, "Mom, when did you get this? May I try it? It smells amazing!" As soon as the words left her lips and she closed her mouth, the three of us froze, locking eyes. I repeated her last sentence, "It smells amazing!" Oh, my cat! Floofy disliked this strong fragrance on her fur. I had switched to a new hand cream, inadvertently leaving the scent on her every time I stroked her. Her obsessive grooming was an attempt to rid herself of the scent. She must have been frustrated with my constant touch throughout the day. No matter how hard she tried to remove the smell, I unknowingly reapplied it. Thus, the cycle persisted. No wonder she tirelessly groomed herself. It was all because of my unwitting actions.

Now we had the answer to the question. But why do cats groom themselves? I did some internet research and found numerous explanations. They groom to keep clean, distribute natural skin oils, stimulate circulation, and more. In essence, it's a self-care ritual—a practice they engage in for their own benefit.

Why do you want to enter the world of self-publishing? Is it the allure of passive income? The desire to escape the nine-to-five grind? Craving more freedom? Yes, it seems like our objectives are clear. We all embark on this journey for ourselves. Understanding this straightforward and obvious goal is crucial, as it shapes our attitude and approach. If doing it for ourselves is our top priority, then we must ensure that we truly enjoy the process. This enjoyment should extend beyond short-term excitement or the allure of monetary rewards. Ultimately, we want to build something that brings us long-term satisfaction and fulfillment.

Have you ever spent time researching a supposedly profitable genre that you lacked passion for? I have. I once invested considerable time exploring the possibility of publishing a series of toddler coloring books. However, I realized it wasn't my forte or passion. The world of adult coloring books, and especially the popular ones with swear words, was another area I explored. Maybe I could handle this, I told myself. Yet, I don't even swear, and Floofy couldn't assist me in that department either. Can you believe I even asked ChatGPT to provide me with a list of swear words for reference? Its reply left me both relieved and grateful. "I apologize, but as an AI developed by OpenAI, I am programmed to follow ethical guidelines, which include promoting positive and respectful communication. I am unable to provide you with explicit or offensive language, including swear words. However, I'd be happy to help you with any other inquiries or assist you with different topics." I must admit, I'm glad ChatGPT refused to aid me in that endeavor. Otherwise, I might have second thoughts about associating my name with such content. After all, I self-publish for myself. I want to share my books with pride among friends and family. I want my works to reflect my true self, to be authentic and original.

What about you? Does this feline wisdom resonate with your own journey?

If doing it for ourselves is our top priority, then we must ensure that we truly enjoy the process. This enjoyment should extend beyond short-term excitement or the allure of monetary rewards.

Enjoying the Process

I believe many of you reading this book are cat lovers, and I'm certain you've witnessed the hilarious spectacle of cats playing with laser pointers. I remember the first time I saw a cat chasing that elusive red dot on an old-fashioned TV program. I couldn't contain my laughter as I watched their unwavering determination.

Curiosity got the better of me, and I pondered why this simple game was so irresistibly captivating to our feline friends. The same shop that delivered Floofy's food and treats also sold laser pointers, so I ordered one, eagerly anticipating the joyous playtime that awaited us.

After a few days of anticipation, the package arrived, and I couldn't wait to unleash the laughter and interactive fun with Floofy. I envisioned her leaping, pouncing, and chasing the red dot with sheer delight. Oh, the joy it brought me just thinking about it!

I was not disappointed. Floofy's excitement was palpable as she energetically engaged in the chase. The red dot became her sworn nemesis, and she was determined to catch and conquer it. I laughed, offering playful encouragement, saying, "Almost there... oh, so close!" But after a few minutes—maybe three, or was it five? I can't recall precisely—Floofy grew tired. Her purr-suit slowed, and eventually, she came to a halt. She looked at my hand holding the laser pointer, raised her head to meet my gaze, and then simply walked away.

I was dumbfounded. It became evident that she knew from the start that the red dot originated from the little contraption I held. She chased it not for the dot itself, but for the joy of playing together. It made me wonder: Was I entertaining Floofy, or was Floofy entertaining me? The answer eludes me, but honestly, I don't mind. Apart from a slight dent in my dignity, I'm perfectly content not knowing.

Ah, but the significance of this revelation goes beyond cat antics—it holds relevance to self-publishing. If success is the red dot and you are the cat, will you tirelessly pursue it, even knowing you may not catch it?

Dear friends, I challenge you to think over this question. As for me, the answer is a resounding yes. Let me share something about myself. I may have failed to mention it before, but I'm not just a self-publisher. I'm also a seasoned executive with decades of experience in making informed decisions. Calculating costs and benefits is practically my second nature. I'm dead serious. Consider this an acid test. Unless you genuinely enjoy the process—metaphorically, chasing the red dot—the potential cost may outweigh the potential gains. And let's face it, how many indie authors and publishers are out there? The numbers are vast, my friends.

Think about it: in a sea of indie authors and publishers, how do you make your books stand out? If everyone is fishing in the same freelancer pool, using the same ghostwriters, editors, and designers, how will your books stand out from the crowd? If everyone's using similar A.I. technologies and those creating low and medium-content books employ similar tools, what sets you apart? If everyone is utilizing the same keyword research tools and methods, what makes you believe your ideas will be superior? You might as well buy a lottery ticket!

Please don't misunderstand me. I remain a firm believer in self-publishing. After all, I'm still writing—yes, this book you're reading was penned by me, not some ghostwriter. But let's be real, if I solely focused on the final sales figure, I probably wouldn't be writing this book. There's no foolproof proof-of-concept or a profitable keyword strategy backing it. However, I'm here because I genuinely enjoy the process. I strongly believe we need our unique voice, our creative spark, and an unyielding determination to entertain and delight readers. Writing this book brings me immense joy and fulfillment, and that's a sure-win in itself.

So, my dear self-publishing comrades, I urge you to reflect on the delightful actions of Floofy and her red-dot chase. Those who are truly passionate about their craft will pursue it with unwavering determination, regardless of the outcome. It's through that wholehearted commitment that you'll find true enjoyment in the journey, and build the resilience needed to weather the challenges along the way. And let's not forget, patience and perseverance are faithful companions to a self-publisher's soul.

Self-publishing can be a wild ride, but it's also a journey filled with satisfaction and fulfillment. So, as you chase your own red dot of success, keep the Floofy spirit alive within you. Embrace the process, laugh in the face of challenges, and remember that the journey is as whimsical as a cat's playful antics, and the rewards are far more than just dollar signs. Happy publishing adventures to you all!

MY CAT BECOMES A SELF-PUBLISHER

> Those who are truly passionate about their craft will pursue it with unwavering determination, regardless of the outcome.

Unleashing Your Unquenchable Hunter Passion

Floofy despises trips to the vet, and I must admit, I share a similar sentiment, albeit for different reasons. The mere sight of her travel cage sends her into a frenzy, with continuous meows echoing through the car ride. It's a symphony of feline anxiety that only subsides once we step foot inside the clinic. I can't help but think that Floofy's vocal cords simply give up on her, leaving her speechless with terror.

Today, Floofy required a visit to the vet due to an upset stomach. She had vomited three times the previous day, which was completely out of the ordinary. Naturally, I couldn't help but worry about what could have caused her distress. Did she eat something unsavory during her daring escapades? It's a mystery because Floofy is incredibly picky when it comes to her food. She won't even stoop so low as to pick up a fallen morsel from the ground. So how in the world did she manage to upset her delicate tummy?

Upon arriving at the clinic, we were greeted by a seasoned, middle-aged veterinarian—a compassionate and gentle soul with a deep affinity for animals. Personally, I held a great fondness for her, but it seemed that Ms. Floofy had an entirely different opinion this time around. Although she remained cooperative, it is likely the looming scent of medicinal potions and the aura of anxiety from other furry patients triggered her apprehension. Though I must say, Floofy used to be a fearless explorer during her kitten days. On previous visits to the vet, she would saunter around as if the clinic were her personal playground. I vividly remember the time she perched herself on the wireless mouse, much to the vet's amusement as she searched high and low for her misplaced gadget.

However, today was a different story. Floofy lay there, as still as a statue, on the examination table. The vet began her check-up, gently pressing and palpating Floofy's rib cage and tummy while asking me a barrage of questions. I relayed the details of Floofy's condition—despite her frequent vomiting episodes, she remained active, and her appetite hadn't diminished. The vet, ever the detective, inquired if Floofy had been on any hunting escapades lately. She suspected that her playful exploits with a sick bird or rodent might have caused her upset stomach. I couldn't help but chuckle at the thought of Floofy's hunting prowess, but I assured the vet that Floofy was indeed an accomplished hunter, although she had never shown any interest in consuming her prey. The vet reassured me, explaining that domestic cats hunt more for amusement than for sustenance. Oh, the brutal reality that I had been dodging—a mind-blowing realization that crushed my fairy-tale vision of Floofy as a sweet, angelic being. Oh, spare me the gory details about my precious feline's murderous tendencies, please!

My disapproval must have been written all over my face because the vet quickly stepped in, assuring me that Floofy's predator instinct was simply part of her feline nature. I needn't feel guilty or dismayed by her hunting inclinations as it was ingrained in her DNA. Well, somehow, I did feel a slight sense of relief, knowing that Floofy's innate hunting skills could act as a line of defense against potential rodent invasions within our humble abode. My friend Kacie recently told me about her terrible experience with rodents, which included major damage to her sewer pipes. Thankfully, Floofy's unwavering commitment to her hunting prowess would never allow such a calamity to befall us.

With a reassuring nod, the vet assured me that Floofy would be just fine with a quick injection and a week's worth of medication. She recommended a soft-food diet for the next three days, with a gradual return to her usual fare if her condition improved. I couldn't help but imagine the sheer delight this temporary change in diet would bring to Floofy's discerning taste buds, as she had always shown a preference for wet food that bordered on obsession.

Speaking of hunting, Floofy pales in comparison to my friend's cat, Coony, a magnificent Maine Coon with a reputation for bringing home a wide array of "prizes." Coony's offerings range from birds to mice, and my friend Judy once regaled me with a story of her mischievous feline even dragging home their neighbor's pet turtle.

The image of a cat triumphantly dragging a turtle in its jaws left me in fits of laughter. The unquenchable desires and primal drives of these feline predators are truly remarkable.

It begs the question: when was the last time you felt such unrelenting passion? Where does your own unquenchable desire lie? In reflecting on the wisdom of our feline friends, I've come to realize that self-publishing, particularly for indie authors who begin their journey as part-timers, requires us to unleash our inner hunters. It is this boundless passion that fuels us, providing us with infinite energy and unwavering perseverance. Even if our writing cannot yet replace our full-time jobs, even if the publishing landscape proves more challenging than anticipated, even if others dismiss our goals as foolish or unattainable, and even if the world doubts our decision to invest our life savings in peripheral services, courses, and products.

The conversation with the vet kept swirling around in my mind: "Floofy hunts for amusement." It made me ponder, what if self-publishing doesn't bring in money? Just like Floofy not being able to hunt for a living, would I still pursue it? I don't have a definite answer. Deep down, I hope to make money from my efforts, and I'm sure you do too. After all, why invest precious time, effort, and hard-earned money if there's no payoff? That goal remains non-negotiable, without a second thought. But the wisdom of cats goes even deeper. The cat's obsession with hunting reminds us to appreciate the journey, to relish the process itself. Before reaching the light at the end of the tunnel, it's the passion that fuels our engine, supporting us to persist through setbacks and hardships, keeping us going even when we encounter obstacles and challenges, like Floofy's epic battle with an upset stomach.

I like to envision self-publishing as a marathon. We can't exhaust ourselves right at the beginning of the journey. We must preserve our strength and endurance, ensuring that we remain passionate throughout. We need to keep our energy levels high and our enthusiasm intact, so we can stay pumped throughout this wild journey! This is what I mean by our unquenchable passion. Let's take inspiration from our feline companions and embrace our own unquenchable desires. May they serve as the catalyst that ignites the flames of our never-ending passion.

Our own unquenchable desires serve as the catalyst that ignites the flames of our never-ending passion.

Building Your Brand

Allow me to take you on a journey down memory lane for just a moment! Back in my university days, I embarked on a wild driving excursion with a merry band of friends. It was an experience I'll never forget. Oh, those were the good old days! Energy in abundance, and time seemed to stretch out forever. But don't worry about me. These days, my physical strength prefers a cozy flight over an extended road trip. Safety first, you know!

Now, let me get to the fishy part of the story! Picture this: a bunch of clueless adventurers, yours truly included, decided to try our hands at fishing during our road trip. No fishing rods? No problem! We had our trusty fishing lines to do the job. Who needs fancy equipment, right?

At the wharf, we stood, looking like three bewildered kids who couldn't tell a hook from a bait. Boredom was creeping in—sun too bright, wind too strong—and we were startled when a cat jumped down from a yacht that was docked nearby and approached us. How could I possibly fathom that there are people living on a yacht with a cat? The cat was sitting there, appearing unperturbed and unruffled. Observing three people who weren't very good at what they were doing as humans. Since the cat didn't appear to be impressed by what we were doing, I have a hunch that its owner must be a skilled angler, given how the cat reacted to what we did. Or was I imagining it?

Then, magic happened. One friend hooked a small fish, and faster than a mouse on roller skates, he tossed it to our newfound yacht cat friend. That day, I was witness to something that was really mind-blowing, and to this day, I can vividly picture what I saw in my mind's eye. With one paw, the large tabby cat held the dancing fish firmly in place on the ground. After that, he cocked his head to one side (I'm going to assume it's a male cat) and bit the head side of the fish, thereby severing it in two. He started gnawing on the fish. The sound that I heard was extremely reminiscent of the sound that I make when munching potato chips—it sounded crunchy. As soon as he completed the upper portion of the fish, he pulled his paw from the other half of the fish and ate that as well.

Suddenly, fishing became a mission. I didn't feel bored anymore. We all wanted to impress our new feline connoisseur! By the end of the day, we had fed him a total of eight fish, and he dined with the grace of royalty at a banquet.

Now, you might think all cats adore fish, but no, at least not my mischievous Floofy! She's a picky eater, turning her nose up at salmon and tuna delights. Only chicken, turkey, and an occasional beef morsel can satisfy her. Maybe that explains her obsession with birds. She's got her own unique style!

It's possible that you're wondering, "What does the moral of this story teach us?" What is a cat's wisdom on this? What I took away from this is the importance of clear differentiation in the work of a writer. You have to stand out from the crowd if you want readers to keep you in their memories. You need a character, either a very unique author profile or a very unique writing style, highly unique themes, and so on, in order to identify yourself from the sea of other writers. To put it another way, we require the establishment of our own brand. We need something that can get readers interested in what we have to say. Think of the cat on the yacht that ate raw fish while it was still alive. After such a long time, I am still able to recall every detail of the scene since it was so remarkable. Even though Floofy is not a very unique cat, the fact that she dislikes seafood makes her somewhat unusual. And speaking of uniqueness, that's the key to being a successful writer. We need to stand out in the vast sea of authors. Just like that yacht cat dining on raw fish, we must be special and different. Create a character, a style, and a plot that leave readers with a lasting impression. Build our brand, my friend!

What's your story? How do you intend to make a connection with the people who read your work? How would you describe yourself in your author profile? Think of yourself as a reader who could be interested. Are you going to find yourself drawn to this author? What sets you apart from others? How would you differentiate yourself from the other writers? In your mind's eye, what does a successful author seem like? Create a plan for that picture, and then start working towards your objective. Write your way to success, just like our yacht cat friend dining in style. The world awaits your literary brilliance!

Just like that yacht cat dining on raw fish, we must be special and different. Create a character, a style, and a plot that leave readers with a lasting impression.

Chapter 6
Choosing Your Battle

"It's crucial to choose your battles wisely. Don't be afraid to pick a fight, but never underestimate the importance of sizing up your opponents."

Floofy – The Vigilant Feline

Picking Your Fight

I'm pretty certain that all cat owners can relate to this: your cat always seems to be the first to notice an intruder, whether it's a pesky fly or a mischievous grasshopper. Floofy is no exception. In fact, I was taken aback the first time I heard her emit that comical noise. It wasn't quite a hiss, more like a dog's bark but softer and higher-pitched. Then I witnessed her leaping, pouncing, and gracefully twirling around, as if performing a feline rendition of the renowned ballet, "Swan Lake." It turned out she was actually chasing a tiny moth. I couldn't be bothered to search the internet to determine whether it was the motion of the moth or the faint sound of fluttering wings that caught her attention. Well, it could have been both, but let's just say I'm too lazy to find out.

One day, a humming noise filled the air. At first, I couldn't pinpoint its source. But as I stepped into the kitchen, the noise grew louder. I noticed a small shadow dancing on the window. Thinking it was just another trapped fly, I had intended to open the window and set the poor insect free. However, Floofy's meows abruptly took on a warning tone—a departure from her usual meow and certainly not the hunting meow that resembled a dog's bark. That's when I knew something was amiss. With caution, I moved closer and discovered it wasn't a fly at all—it was a wasp. It took me a moment to figure out what to do, but eventually,

MY CAT BECOMES A SELF-PUBLISHER

I managed to free the wasp by opening all nearby windows. The wasp left, and Floofy and I emerged unscathed.

Once I regained my composure, a question nagged at me: "How did Floofy sense the unwelcome presence? Had she been stung by a wasp before?" I couldn't recall any signs of her being stung or experiencing abnormal insect bites. Could it be an animal instinct—an ability to discern risk from opportunity? My mind wandered as I contemplated this notion.

Then another incident sprung to mind. One day when I was engrossed in my chores—what exactly I was doing escapes me—I overheard an intense screeching noise that I was certain signaled an animal altercation. Initially, I didn't pay it much heed, until I realized Floofy was nowhere to be found. Worried, I stepped out through the French doors of the dining room and followed the noise. As I approached the fence that separated my house from my neighbor's, the commotion grew louder. Fearful that something terrible had transpired, I called out Floofy's name with all the volume I could muster. Suddenly, the noise ceased, and around five seconds later, Floofy bounded over the fence. The fur along her back stood on end, and her tail fluffed up, appearing even more magnificent than usual. She emitted throaty noises that, to me, sounded like a string of colorful expletives. Do cats swear? I had no idea until that day.

It was a sight I hadn't seen before—a ferocity in Floofy that contradicted her delicate and fragile nature. A visiting friend with a toddler could send her fleeing in milliseconds. Dogs? No way. The barks of a dog even roughly her size would send her scurrying home in a flash. Drop a pen on the floor, and she'd dash away in a comical blur. It always amused me to see her feet move at a frenetic pace, almost like she was paddling in place, while her claws desperately scrabbled against the uncarpeted floor, achieving no forward movement.

How does Floofy choose her battles? This question lingered so I asked Floofy directly, "How do you discern danger from fun? How do you differentiate between hazard and pleasure? Is it an innate trait, encoded within your DNA?" Floofy didn't respond with meows but instead twinkled her eyes, offering two slow blinks—a signal that it was time for the wise cat philosopher to share her wisdom. So, I continued my profound musings.

Suddenly, Floofy playfully nipped at my pant leg, a clear signal that it was time for her supper. I glanced at her, understanding that she doesn't engage in a fight unless she has confidence in securing the upper hand. Look at what she has just done to me. She was not afraid as she knew I wouldn't hurt her. For other potential threats, she is vigilant and won't risk getting hurt unnecessarily.

To apply this feline wisdom to self-publishing, we, too, must choose our battles wisely. Beyond potential profitability, we must assess our chances of success, such as the competition and the number of big players in a particular niche. Our resources are limited—our time, effort, and money are finite. Therefore, we must carefully select our fights and avoid engaging in activities where our chances of victory are slim. This is particularly crucial when we are starting out, without an established fan base and relying purely on personal savings.

Ouch! My ankle received another, slightly firmer nip. I looked at Floofy, who displayed a hint of impatience. Alright, I understood. It was time to reward our esteemed content contributor—the great feline philosopher, Floofy. After all, you can't expect a hungry soldier to win a battle. I dashed toward the cupboard where her cat food was kept. Floofy closely trailed behind me, her rhythmic meows harmonizing perfectly with my footsteps.

Our resources are limited—our time, effort, and money are finite. Therefore, we must carefully select our fights and avoid engaging in activities where our chances of victory are slim.

Recharging and Restoring

It was my turn to fall victim to the dreaded sickness. My throat felt as scratchy as a cat's post-scratch pole, and I was as weak as a newborn kitten. My first move was to do a Rapid Test. Phew! Only one line appeared. It was a Saturday, and I had zero desire to leave the house. I rummaged through the first aid kit and discovered a stash of paracetamol. Not just a few, but enough to make a pill pyramid. Although I didn't have a headache, I popped two tablets just for the heck of it. Who knows, maybe they held the secret to some grand myth. I reasoned that even if they couldn't cure me, they certainly wouldn't do any harm. Better safe than sorry, right?

Back in my study, I opened my manuscript, the very one you're currently reading. The book was more than halfway complete, and I was buzzing with excitement, eagerly anticipating the finish line. But, alas, my mind betrayed me, refusing to cooperate and slamming shut like a bank vault door.

I sat in front of the computer, my mind adrift like a feather in the wind. I opened my browser, browsing the latest news without much interest in reading them. I checked my email, combing through all my inboxes. I even logged into my KDP account, staring at the dashboard, performing all the rituals except praying to the elusive KDP God (because, let's face it, they don't exist). Self-publishing demands dedication, devotion, and hard work—not some stroke of heavenly luck. Oh no, my mind had slipped away again!

Determined to refocus, I scolded myself. How could I give up on this sacred Saturday, a day solely dedicated to my writing? It's a precious gift, one that comes around only once a week. Frustration began to devour my sanity. Desperately seeking inspiration, my eyes wandered around the room. Where was my co-author, Floofy? I called out her name, waited for a dramatic pause of five seconds, and to my disappointment, all I received was complete silence.

Seizing the opportunity, I made my way to the kitchen to return my empty coffee cup, keeping an eye out for Floofy along the way. As I stepped into the sunlit dining room, a revelation struck me. Yes, Floofy was outside, but she wasn't frolicking about like a feline on a mission. No, my dear readers, she was sound asleep.

There, in the semi-outdoor area that bridged the dining room and the wooden deck, Floofy had claimed her throne—the middle bar stool of the covered deck. It was a space I whimsically referred to as my outdoor bar, even though it was primarily used for air-drying clothes that couldn't handle the dryer's heat. To add a touch of charm, I had placed three bar stools there, but truth be told, no one in the family had ever sat on them. Or so I thought. Today, I discovered that one family member, Floofy herself, had made herself quite comfortable. She snoozed peacefully atop the middle one, basking in the shaded sunlight. What a waste! Today was a sunny day, the ground was finally dry after a week of rain. "Come on, Floofy, rise and shine! It's playtime!" I silently pleaded, hoping to see some feline enthusiasm.

I left my coffee cup in the sink unwashed, and then hurriedly returned to my study to grab my phone. I had intended to capture some adorable photos of Floofy, documenting this precious moment. You see, I had plans to create a supplementary book to this one, and I needed some captivating snapshots. However, by the time I retrieved my phone and stealthily approached Floofy, she had already awoken. With a stretch and a yawn, she followed me back into the house. Soon enough, she joined me in the study, curling up in a cozy spot for yet another cat nap.

Curiosity piqued; I took to the internet to investigate. Apparently, cats sleep an average of 12 to 16 hours a day. They find solace in slumber, using it to recharge their batteries and boost their immune systems. Cats, unlike us mere mortals burdened with the constant quest for making a living, seem to have passed down the wisdom of appreciating the inherent value of sleep across generations. So, the question remains: Are cats sleeping too much, or are we simply not sleeping enough?

Though I don't have the answer to that thought-provoking question, I do know that traditional values teach us the importance of knowledge, reliability, and consistency in achieving success. There's no denying the value of those virtues, but I propose adding a layer of self-care or self-compassion. After all, we are flesh and blood, and we need to feel good, to be in good shape, in order to be productive. Pushing ourselves to the limit without respite can only lead to burnout. To maintain accuracy and razor-sharp instincts, we must learn to recharge and restore.

Let us learn from our feline gurus, my friends. Let us prioritize our well-being, recognizing the power of downtime. We all require those moments of reset before we pounce again. It's akin to an electrocardiogram, where every summit is preceded by a valley. Never underestimate the importance of rest—our gateway to recharge and restore.

As I glance around, Floofy has pulled off the greatest disappearing act since Houdini. As I sneak a peek through the window, I spot her luxuriously soaking up the sun on the deck like a lizard on vacation. I performed the sacred ritual of clicking "save" and bid a tender farewell to my laptop, gently closing its case as if tucking it in for a cozy nap. I made the brilliant decision to gift myself with a generous serving of "horizontal time" today.

We need to feel good, to be in good shape, in order to be productive. Pushing ourselves to the limit without respite can only lead to burnout.

Herding Cats and Dogs

These days, I found myself immersed in a dog training program on YouTube. It's absolutely captivating to witness the array of dog breeds, selectively bred to assist humanity in various tasks—guiding, herding, hunting, and so much more. According to the Cat Fanciers' Association, there are 45 distinct breeds of cats. However, when it comes to dogs, the numbers skyrocket to anywhere between 190 to 340 breeds, depending on which source you consult.

Dogs encompass an astonishing range of sizes, coat lengths, body shapes, and face shapes, not to mention their diverse temperaments. Their unique qualities and unwavering loyalty make them invaluable in countless endeavors, from supporting law enforcement to detecting explosives and even combating drug smuggling. On the other paw, our feline friends primarily serve as companions, or at most, expert pest controllers.

Talking about loyalty, let me defend our purrfectly loyal feline friends. While some may argue that dogs take the crown in the loyalty department, I'm here to give cats the recognition they deserve. Oh, those sneaky little creatures also have loyalty, just in their own quirky way. But let's be real, dogs are like the Swiss Army knives of a super butler, always ready to lend a paw and save the day. When it comes to cats, their main job is to be your furry friend.

MY CAT BECOMES A SELF-PUBLISHER

But dogs? They go above and beyond! They're like your personal assistant, therapist, and security officer all in one. Need someone to fetch your slippers? They've got you covered. Feeling down? They'll give you cuddles and slobbery kisses. Dogs truly know how to overachieve in the job of being your best buddy. Oh, wait a minute, I remain a loyal cat's fan.

As my internet search continues, I uncover that cats display less heterogeneity compared to dogs. In other words, cats tend to have similar shapes, forms, and sizes. Their temperaments also lean towards independence, self-sufficiency, and reservedness. Dogs, on the other paw, are inherently sociable creatures. While it's clear that dogs hold a significant advantage over cats based purely on their characteristics, a deeper exploration reveals an interesting fact. In 2023, there are estimated to be 900 million dogs and 600 million cats worldwide. If dogs bring so much more value to humanity, why are there still so many cats in the world? If cats weren't as valuable as dogs, they wouldn't have become the second most popular pet. They must possess their own unique value.

Lost in my musings, I glanced at my furry friend who was fervently kneading the mini cushion I had gifted her. She purred while enjoying her moment. To me, seeing her so happy, for an act as simple as that made me rejoice. After kneading the mini-cushion, Floofy curled herself and closed her eyes. I was engaging in deep thoughts, feeling thankful to Floofy's inspiration and wisdom that have just contributed to another paragraph. My thought adrift and I must have stared at her for too long. Cats' instinct kicked in and she opened her eyes, as if sensed my unnecessary attention and awkwardness. As our eyes locked, she responded to me with a dramatic double blink, as if she were auditioning for a slow-motion scene in a romantic movie. How sugary and curative. My heart felt warm, like a cozy little fireplace in the middle of a snowstorm, cranking up the heat in my room by a whopping two degrees.

I believe I've stumbled upon yet another nugget of self-publishing wisdom! Picture this: there are two distinct reader groups in the magical realm of the book market—the mighty "problem-solvers" and the whimsical "fun-seekers". I have been researching self-publishing skills and techniques and watching a lot of online videos. Today, I found myself donning a pair of enchanted glasses that revealed a whole new perspective. For people who read books to figure out how to solve problems, authors need to make books that help people solve their problems. The key to being successful is to offer a solution that is either better than your competitor's, takes less work, or gets results faster. In other words, everyone needs to find their own "competitive edge". Even better, if you can come up with an answer that no one else has come up with before, then you will have an "absolute advantage" over everyone else. By doing that, you reach a market that hasn't been reached yet. I compared

MY CAT BECOMES A SELF-PUBLISHER

it to how "dogs" help people as working dogs. Authors do that to help readers solve problems and show our worth and utility.

Asking whether high-content nonfiction books or medium-content activity books are better is like asking whether dogs or cats are better. There's no easy way to answer this. Many people buy books to find answers to problems, while others do it just for fun, entertainment, and the pure joy of reading. Because of this, there are a lot of romance books, sci-fi epics, thrilling mysteries, and spine-chilling horror stories and many different genres. Even the wave of medium-content activity books falls into this group. These books are for fun and entertainment and have a huge market share. I compare it to cats, whose sole purpose is to make people happy and keep them company and that is as simple as that.

Do you know your destiny yet? It's not a simple yes or no question. You can explore both avenues, especially since self-publishing offers a low-cost entry point. We can develop a low or medium-content book at close to zero cost, but remember, the market is fiercely competitive. Consider it this way: it's competitive because it attracts numerous players, and it attracts numerous players because it's profitable.

We don't need to choose between being dog lovers or cat enthusiasts. The market is vast, leaving ample room for new publishers. The key is to ensure we provide quality products. Just like a household that can accommodate both dogs and cats, the publishing world welcomes diversity and variety.

I gazed at the majestic sight of Floofy's purrfectly coiled fluffitude. She was snoozing away, being my trusty sidekick on this chilly winter night.

Asking whether high-content nonfiction books or medium-content activity books are better is like asking whether dogs or cats are better. There's no easy way to answer this.

Conclusion

Dear fellow writer and self-publisher,

As I reach the end of this book, my heart overflows with gratitude and warmth. I can't help but contemplate the genre this book might fit into, but you know what? It doesn't really matter because what truly matters is the connection we've forged on this incredible journey together.

When I first set foot into the world of self-publishing, I thought it would be a solitary endeavor, just me and my words. Little did I know that this path would lead me to the embrace of a supportive and encouraging community. Along the way, we've connected through social media, online forums, and various tools and services, making us an indispensable part of each other's writing journey. The realization that there are many of us walking this road together fills me with profound gratitude. Thank you for being an essential part of this wonderful community.

Now, as you read this conclusion, it means you've been with me every step of the way, from the very first page to this emotional end. Your presence and support have been a guiding light, and I can't thank you enough for that. Together, we've ventured into the uncharted realms of self-publishing, embracing curiosity and tenacity, just like our feline friends do.

This book marks the beginning of the Kittenpreneur Series, and my dream is to foster a network of kindred souls, like you, who share a love for writing and a passion for cats. I hope you'll join me in this endeavor because, let's face it, there's something magical about these furry companions, something that fills our hearts with joy and our minds with inspiration.

Words possess an immense power—they connect hearts, heal souls, uplift spirits, and transform lives. As authors and self-publishers, we wield this power with each tale we tell, bridging the gaps between cultures and generations, leaving a lasting impact on those who read our words. It's an honor to know that our stories have the potential to bring joy and meaning to the lives of others.

My intention in crafting this book was straightforward and pure. I didn't set out with the goal of chasing bestseller lists or fame. Instead, my heart's desire was to connect with kindred spirits like you, fellow writers and self-publishers who share a love for felines and an appreciation for authenticity.

As you continue on your writing journey, may you be blessed with boundless happiness, prosperity, and a never-ending flow of creative ideas. Each step you take on this path should bring you revelations of joy and meaningful connections with your readers. May your words continue to weave tales that touch hearts and inspire minds, just as the heartwarming stories of Floofy have touched ours.

And remember, this is not a farewell. It's a "see you later" because I have no doubt that our paths will cross again in this vast and wondrous universe of words. So keep writing, keep dreaming, and keep embracing the feline wisdom that has found its way into our lives.

If you'd like to continue this adventure together, I welcome you to sign up for my email list and claim your bonus read. Let's stay connected, share our thoughts, gain new perspectives, and inspire each other on this writing journey. Together, we are stronger, braver, and more resilient—just like the feline inspirations that have guided us.

From the depths of my heart, I want to express my gratitude for joining me on this journey. May your days be filled with the enchantment of storytelling and the soothing purrs of inspiration until we meet again. Until then, I wish you much success and fulfillment in all your writing endeavors.

With warmest regards and endless appreciation,

Winnie & Floofy

P.S. Your review means the world to me and Floofy!

Leave a review on Amazon US

Leave a review on Amazon UK

MY CAT BECOMES A SELF-PUBLISHER

About the Author

Hello there! I'm Winnie Fontaine. I hold a master's degree in commerce, but my journey began as a flight attendant, where I saved up to make my university dream come true.

With sheer determination, I graduated with my master's degree with a scholarship, and that changed my life! From there, I climbed up the corporate ladder and proudly wore the VP hat, specializing in communications and public relations. I am also a leadership coach. But life had more surprises. In 2022, I made the daring choice to be a stay-at-home mom. That's when I discovered my love for writing, something I'd always dreamed of.

I consider myself cheerful, warm, and straightforward, with a playful touch. I don't waste time on people who don't appreciate me. Life's too short to worry about that stuff! My writing style reflects just that—genuine, heartfelt, and maybe a bit witty, as some say.

Welcome to my world—the "Kittenpreneur Series". I'm pumped to share my stories with you, and I promise they'll bring some sunshine and inspiration your way. Take care and keep smiling, my friend!

Calling for ARC Readers

Dear friends,

ARC stands for Advance Review Copy. Floofy and I are truly amazed by your incredible support. Would you like to read our upcoming story before its release—for free? All you need to do is to send an email to cats.wisdom@soulspress.com with the subject heading: ARC

As an emerging author, building a fan base is crucial to us. If you enjoyed this book, we warmly invite you to join Floofy and me. We're dedicated to crafting new books that bring joy, fun, and life wisdom to our readers. By joining our ARC list, you'll stay informed about our latest releases and be the first to read our new works. We can't wait to have you on board.

Yours truly,
Winnie and Floofy

Bonus Page

This is a friendly reminder that I have prepared a set of bonus gifts for you.

As an expression of gratitude for your purchase, I would like to offer you a bonus read, a couple of Floofy's stories, her philosophical quotes, and some photos that have not been shared before. These valuable resources are dedicated to all my respectful readers. Scan the QR code or you may visit this website:

https://soulspress.com/opt-in-page-cats-wisdom

References

Bright Side (2021, May 24). Why We Have 190 Dog Breeds but Only 42 Cat Types. https://www.youtube.com/watch?v=OXChj9wp-V0

Ljubica Kvitova. (2023 UPDATE). 61 Fun Cat Statistics That Are the Cat's Meow!

The Cat Fanciers Association. (2023, July 17). Breed Characteristics and Personalities. https://cfa.org/kids/breeds-and-colors/cfa-breeds/

Wonderopolis. (2023, July 16). Why Are There More Different Types of Dogs Than There Are Cats?

https://www.wonderopolis.org/wonder/why-are-there-more-different-types-of-dogs-than-there-are-cats#:~:text=According%20to%20the%20Cat%20Fanciers,to%20the%20World%20Canine%20Organization

www.ingramcontent.com/pod-product-compliance
Lightning Source LLC
Chambersburg PA
CBHW031120080526
44587CB00011B/1055